AF887974

WEEKLY BUDGET TRACKER

THIS BOOK BELONGS TO

Saving Goal

52 Week Savings Challenge

WEEK	AMOUNT DEPOSITED	AMOUNT BALANCE	WEEK	AMOUNT DEPOSITED	AMOUNT BALANCE
1	$1.00	$1.00	27	$27.00	$378.00
2	$2.00	$3.00	28	$28.00	$406.00
3	$3.00	$6.00	29	$29.00	$435.00
4	$4.00	$10.00	30	$30.00	$465.00
5	$5.00	$15.00	31	$31.00	$496.00
6	$6.00	$21.00	32	$32.00	$528.00
7	$7.00	$28.00	33	$33.00	$561.00
8	$8.00	$36.00	34	$34.00	$595.00
9	$9.00	$45.00	35	$35.00	$630.00
10	$10.00	$55.00	36	$36.00	$666.00
11	$11.00	$66.00	37	$37.00	$703.00
12	$12.00	$78.00	38	$38.00	$741.00
13	$13.00	$91.00	39	$39.00	$780.00
14	$14.00	$105.00	40	$40.00	$820.00
15	$15.00	$120.00	41	$41.00	$861.00
16	$16.00	$136.00	42	$42.00	$903.00
17	$17.00	$153.00	43	$43.00	$946.00
18	$18.00	$171.00	44	$44.00	$990.00
19	$19.00	$190.00	45	$45.00	$1035.00
20	$20.00	$210.00	46	$46.00	$1081.00
21	$21.00	$231.00	47	$47.00	$1128.00
22	$22.00	$253.00	48	$48.00	$1176.00
23	$23.00	$276.00	49	$49.00	$1225.00
24	$24.00	$300.00	50	$50.00	$1275.00
25	$25.00	$325.00	51	$51.00	$1326.00
26	$26.00	$351.00	52	$52.00	$1378.00

Notes

WEEKLY BUDGET TRACKER

WEEK OF:

MONDAY	
DESCRIPTION	AMOUNT
TOTAL $	

TUESDAY	
DESCRIPTION	AMOUNT
TOTAL $	

WEDNESDAY	
DESCRIPTION	AMOUNT
TOTAL $	

THURSDAY	
DESCRIPTION	AMOUNT
TOTAL $	

FRIDAY	
DESCRIPTION	AMOUNT
TOTAL $	

SATURDAY	
DESCRIPTION	AMOUNT
TOTAL $	

SUNDAY	
DESCRIPTION	AMOUNT
TOTAL $	

NOTES

AMOUNT TO SPEND
$
SPENT
$
SAVINGS
$
LEFT OVER AMOUNT
$

WEEKLY BUDGET TRACKER

WEEK OF:

MONDAY	
DESCRIPTION	AMOUNT
TOTAL $	

TUESDAY	
DESCRIPTION	AMOUNT
TOTAL $	

WEDNESDAY	
DESCRIPTION	AMOUNT
TOTAL $	

THURSDAY	
DESCRIPTION	AMOUNT
TOTAL $	

FRIDAY	
DESCRIPTION	AMOUNT
TOTAL $	

SATURDAY	
DESCRIPTION	AMOUNT
TOTAL $	

SUNDAY	
DESCRIPTION	AMOUNT
TOTAL $	

NOTES

AMOUNT TO SPEND
$
SPENT
$
SAVINGS
$
LEFT OVER AMOUNT
$

WEEKLY BUDGET TRACKER

WEEK OF:

MONDAY	
DESCRIPTION	AMOUNT
TOTAL $	

TUESDAY	
DESCRIPTION	AMOUNT
TOTAL $	

WEDNESDAY	
DESCRIPTION	AMOUNT
TOTAL $	

THURSDAY	
DESCRIPTION	AMOUNT
TOTAL $	

FRIDAY

DESCRIPTION	AMOUNT
TOTAL $	

SATURDAY

DESCRIPTION	AMOUNT
TOTAL $	

SUNDAY

DESCRIPTION	AMOUNT
TOTAL $	

NOTES

AMOUNT TO SPEND
$
SPENT
$
SAVINGS
$
LEFT OVER AMOUNT
$

WEEKLY BUDGET TRACKER

WEEK OF:

MONDAY	
DESCRIPTION	AMOUNT
TOTAL $	

TUESDAY	
DESCRIPTION	AMOUNT
TOTAL $	

WEDNESDAY	
DESCRIPTION	AMOUNT
TOTAL $	

THURSDAY	
DESCRIPTION	AMOUNT
TOTAL $	

FRIDAY

DESCRIPTION	AMOUNT
TOTAL $	

SATURDAY

DESCRIPTION	AMOUNT
TOTAL $	

SUNDAY

DESCRIPTION	AMOUNT
TOTAL $	

NOTES

AMOUNT TO SPEND
$
SPENT
$
SAVINGS
$
LEFT OVER AMOUNT
$

WEEKLY BUDGET TRACKER

WEEK OF:

MONDAY	
DESCRIPTION	AMOUNT
TOTAL $	

TUESDAY	
DESCRIPTION	AMOUNT
TOTAL $	

WEDNESDAY	
DESCRIPTION	AMOUNT
TOTAL $	

THURSDAY	
DESCRIPTION	AMOUNT
TOTAL $	

FRIDAY

DESCRIPTION	AMOUNT
TOTAL $	

SATURDAY

DESCRIPTION	AMOUNT
TOTAL $	

SUNDAY

DESCRIPTION	AMOUNT
TOTAL $	

NOTES

AMOUNT TO SPEND
$
SPENT
$
SAVINGS
$
LEFT OVER AMOUNT
$

WEEKLY BUDGET TRACKER

WEEK OF:

MONDAY

DESCRIPTION	AMOUNT
TOTAL $	

TUESDAY

DESCRIPTION	AMOUNT
TOTAL $	

WEDNESDAY

DESCRIPTION	AMOUNT
TOTAL $	

THURSDAY

DESCRIPTION	AMOUNT
TOTAL $	

FRIDAY	
DESCRIPTION	AMOUNT
TOTAL $	

SATURDAY	
DESCRIPTION	AMOUNT
TOTAL $	

SUNDAY	
DESCRIPTION	AMOUNT
TOTAL $	

NOTES

AMOUNT TO SPEND
$
SPENT
$
SAVINGS
$
LEFT OVER AMOUNT
$

WEEKLY BUDGET TRACKER

WEEK OF:

MONDAY	
DESCRIPTION	AMOUNT
TOTAL $	

TUESDAY	
DESCRIPTION	AMOUNT
TOTAL $	

WEDNESDAY	
DESCRIPTION	AMOUNT
TOTAL $	

THURSDAY	
DESCRIPTION	AMOUNT
TOTAL $	

FRIDAY	
DESCRIPTION	AMOUNT
TOTAL $	

SATURDAY	
DESCRIPTION	AMOUNT
TOTAL $	

SUNDAY	
DESCRIPTION	AMOUNT
TOTAL $	

NOTES

AMOUNT TO SPEND
$
SPENT
$
SAVINGS
$
LEFT OVER AMOUNT
$

WEEKLY BUDGET TRACKER

WEEK OF:

MONDAY	
DESCRIPTION	AMOUNT
TOTAL $	

TUESDAY	
DESCRIPTION	AMOUNT
TOTAL $	

WEDNESDAY	
DESCRIPTION	AMOUNT
TOTAL $	

THURSDAY	
DESCRIPTION	AMOUNT
TOTAL $	

FRIDAY

DESCRIPTION	AMOUNT
TOTAL $	

SATURDAY

DESCRIPTION	AMOUNT
TOTAL $	

SUNDAY

DESCRIPTION	AMOUNT
TOTAL $	

NOTES

AMOUNT TO SPEND
$
SPENT
$
SAVINGS
$
LEFT OVER AMOUNT
$

WEEKLY BUDGET TRACKER

WEEK OF:

MONDAY

DESCRIPTION	AMOUNT
TOTAL $	

TUESDAY

DESCRIPTION	AMOUNT
TOTAL $	

WEDNESDAY

DESCRIPTION	AMOUNT
TOTAL $	

THURSDAY

DESCRIPTION	AMOUNT
TOTAL $	

FRIDAY	
DESCRIPTION	AMOUNT
TOTAL $	

SATURDAY	
DESCRIPTION	AMOUNT
TOTAL $	

SUNDAY	
DESCRIPTION	AMOUNT
TOTAL $	

NOTES

AMOUNT TO SPEND
$
SPENT
$
SAVINGS
$
LEFT OVER AMOUNT
$

WEEKLY BUDGET TRACKER

WEEK OF:

MONDAY	
DESCRIPTION	AMOUNT
TOTAL $	

TUESDAY	
DESCRIPTION	AMOUNT
TOTAL $	

WEDNESDAY	
DESCRIPTION	AMOUNT
TOTAL $	

THURSDAY	
DESCRIPTION	AMOUNT
TOTAL $	

FRIDAY	
DESCRIPTION	AMOUNT
TOTAL $	

SATURDAY	
DESCRIPTION	AMOUNT
TOTAL $	

SUNDAY	
DESCRIPTION	AMOUNT
TOTAL $	

NOTES

AMOUNT TO SPEND
$
SPENT
$
SAVINGS
$
LEFT OVER AMOUNT
$

WEEKLY BUDGET TRACKER

WEEK OF:

MONDAY	
DESCRIPTION	AMOUNT
TOTAL $	

TUESDAY	
DESCRIPTION	AMOUNT
TOTAL $	

WEDNESDAY	
DESCRIPTION	AMOUNT
TOTAL $	

THURSDAY	
DESCRIPTION	AMOUNT
TOTAL $	

FRIDAY	
DESCRIPTION	AMOUNT
TOTAL $	

SATURDAY	
DESCRIPTION	AMOUNT
TOTAL $	

SUNDAY	
DESCRIPTION	AMOUNT
TOTAL $	

NOTES

AMOUNT TO SPEND
$
SPENT
$
SAVINGS
$
LEFT OVER AMOUNT
$

WEEKLY BUDGET TRACKER

WEEK OF:

MONDAY

DESCRIPTION	AMOUNT
TOTAL $	

TUESDAY

DESCRIPTION	AMOUNT
TOTAL $	

WEDNESDAY

DESCRIPTION	AMOUNT
TOTAL $	

THURSDAY

DESCRIPTION	AMOUNT
TOTAL $	

FRIDAY	
DESCRIPTION	AMOUNT
TOTAL $	

SATURDAY	
DESCRIPTION	AMOUNT
TOTAL $	

SUNDAY	
DESCRIPTION	AMOUNT
TOTAL $	

NOTES

AMOUNT TO SPEND
$
SPENT
$
SAVINGS
$
LEFT OVER AMOUNT
$

WEEKLY BUDGET TRACKER

WEEK OF:

MONDAY	
DESCRIPTION	AMOUNT
TOTAL $	

TUESDAY	
DESCRIPTION	AMOUNT
TOTAL $	

WEDNESDAY	
DESCRIPTION	AMOUNT
TOTAL $	

THURSDAY	
DESCRIPTION	AMOUNT
TOTAL $	

FRIDAY

DESCRIPTION	AMOUNT
TOTAL $	

SATURDAY

DESCRIPTION	AMOUNT
TOTAL $	

SUNDAY

DESCRIPTION	AMOUNT
TOTAL $	

NOTES

AMOUNT TO SPEND
$
SPENT
$
SAVINGS
$
LEFT OVER AMOUNT
$

WEEKLY BUDGET TRACKER

WEEK OF:

MONDAY	
DESCRIPTION	AMOUNT
TOTAL $	

TUESDAY	
DESCRIPTION	AMOUNT
TOTAL $	

WEDNESDAY	
DESCRIPTION	AMOUNT
TOTAL $	

THURSDAY	
DESCRIPTION	AMOUNT
TOTAL $	

FRIDAY	
DESCRIPTION	AMOUNT
TOTAL $	

SATURDAY	
DESCRIPTION	AMOUNT
TOTAL $	

SUNDAY	
DESCRIPTION	AMOUNT
TOTAL $	

NOTES

AMOUNT TO SPEND
$
SPENT
$
SAVINGS
$
LEFT OVER AMOUNT
$

WEEKLY BUDGET TRACKER

WEEK OF:

MONDAY	
DESCRIPTION	AMOUNT
TOTAL $	

TUESDAY	
DESCRIPTION	AMOUNT
TOTAL $	

WEDNESDAY	
DESCRIPTION	AMOUNT
TOTAL $	

THURSDAY	
DESCRIPTION	AMOUNT
TOTAL $	

FRIDAY	
DESCRIPTION	AMOUNT
TOTAL $	

SATURDAY	
DESCRIPTION	AMOUNT
TOTAL $	

SUNDAY	
DESCRIPTION	AMOUNT
TOTAL $	

NOTES

AMOUNT TO SPEND
$
SPENT
$
SAVINGS
$
LEFT OVER AMOUNT
$

WEEKLY BUDGET TRACKER

WEEK OF:

MONDAY	
DESCRIPTION	AMOUNT
TOTAL $	

TUESDAY	
DESCRIPTION	AMOUNT
TOTAL $	

WEDNESDAY	
DESCRIPTION	AMOUNT
TOTAL $	

THURSDAY	
DESCRIPTION	AMOUNT
TOTAL $	

FRIDAY

DESCRIPTION	AMOUNT
TOTAL $	

SATURDAY

DESCRIPTION	AMOUNT
TOTAL $	

SUNDAY

DESCRIPTION	AMOUNT
TOTAL $	

NOTES

AMOUNT TO SPEND
$
SPENT
$
SAVINGS
$
LEFT OVER AMOUNT
$

WEEKLY BUDGET TRACKER

WEEK OF:

MONDAY

DESCRIPTION	AMOUNT
TOTAL $	

TUESDAY

DESCRIPTION	AMOUNT
TOTAL $	

WEDNESDAY

DESCRIPTION	AMOUNT
TOTAL $	

THURSDAY

DESCRIPTION	AMOUNT
TOTAL $	

FRIDAY

DESCRIPTION	AMOUNT
TOTAL $	

SATURDAY

DESCRIPTION	AMOUNT
TOTAL $	

SUNDAY

DESCRIPTION	AMOUNT
TOTAL $	

NOTES

AMOUNT TO SPEND
$
SPENT
$
SAVINGS
$
LEFT OVER AMOUNT
$

WEEKLY BUDGET TRACKER

WEEK OF:

MONDAY	
DESCRIPTION	AMOUNT
TOTAL $	

TUESDAY	
DESCRIPTION	AMOUNT
TOTAL $	

WEDNESDAY	
DESCRIPTION	AMOUNT
TOTAL $	

THURSDAY	
DESCRIPTION	AMOUNT
TOTAL $	

FRIDAY	
DESCRIPTION	AMOUNT
TOTAL $	

SATURDAY	
DESCRIPTION	AMOUNT
TOTAL $	

SUNDAY	
DESCRIPTION	AMOUNT
TOTAL $	

NOTES

AMOUNT TO SPEND
$
SPENT
$
SAVINGS
$
LEFT OVER AMOUNT
$

WEEKLY BUDGET TRACKER

WEEK OF:

MONDAY	
DESCRIPTION	AMOUNT
TOTAL $	

TUESDAY	
DESCRIPTION	AMOUNT
TOTAL $	

WEDNESDAY	
DESCRIPTION	AMOUNT
TOTAL $	

THURSDAY	
DESCRIPTION	AMOUNT
TOTAL $	

FRIDAY	
DESCRIPTION	AMOUNT
TOTAL $	

SATURDAY	
DESCRIPTION	AMOUNT
TOTAL $	

SUNDAY	
DESCRIPTION	AMOUNT
TOTAL $	

NOTES

AMOUNT TO SPEND
$
SPENT
$
SAVINGS
$
LEFT OVER AMOUNT
$

WEEKLY BUDGET TRACKER

WEEK OF:

MONDAY

DESCRIPTION	AMOUNT
TOTAL $	

TUESDAY

DESCRIPTION	AMOUNT
TOTAL $	

WEDNESDAY

DESCRIPTION	AMOUNT
TOTAL $	

THURSDAY

DESCRIPTION	AMOUNT
TOTAL $	

FRIDAY

DESCRIPTION	AMOUNT
TOTAL $	

SATURDAY

DESCRIPTION	AMOUNT
TOTAL $	

SUNDAY

DESCRIPTION	AMOUNT
TOTAL $	

NOTES

AMOUNT TO SPEND
$
SPENT
$
SAVINGS
$
LEFT OVER AMOUNT
$

WEEKLY BUDGET TRACKER

WEEK OF:

MONDAY	
DESCRIPTION	AMOUNT
TOTAL $	

TUESDAY	
DESCRIPTION	AMOUNT
TOTAL $	

WEDNESDAY	
DESCRIPTION	AMOUNT
TOTAL $	

THURSDAY	
DESCRIPTION	AMOUNT
TOTAL $	

FRIDAY

DESCRIPTION	AMOUNT
TOTAL $	

SATURDAY

DESCRIPTION	AMOUNT
TOTAL $	

SUNDAY

DESCRIPTION	AMOUNT
TOTAL $	

NOTES

AMOUNT TO SPEND
$
SPENT
$
SAVINGS
$
LEFT OVER AMOUNT
$

WEEKLY BUDGET TRACKER

WEEK OF:

MONDAY

DESCRIPTION	AMOUNT
TOTAL $	

TUESDAY

DESCRIPTION	AMOUNT
TOTAL $	

WEDNESDAY

DESCRIPTION	AMOUNT
TOTAL $	

THURSDAY

DESCRIPTION	AMOUNT
TOTAL $	

FRIDAY	
DESCRIPTION	AMOUNT
TOTAL $	

SATURDAY	
DESCRIPTION	AMOUNT
TOTAL $	

SUNDAY	
DESCRIPTION	AMOUNT
TOTAL $	

NOTES

AMOUNT TO SPEND
$
SPENT
$
SAVINGS
$
LEFT OVER AMOUNT
$

WEEKLY BUDGET TRACKER

WEEK OF:

MONDAY	
DESCRIPTION	AMOUNT
TOTAL $	

TUESDAY	
DESCRIPTION	AMOUNT
TOTAL $	

WEDNESDAY	
DESCRIPTION	AMOUNT
TOTAL $	

THURSDAY	
DESCRIPTION	AMOUNT
TOTAL $	

FRIDAY	
DESCRIPTION	AMOUNT
TOTAL $	

SATURDAY	
DESCRIPTION	AMOUNT
TOTAL $	

SUNDAY	
DESCRIPTION	AMOUNT
TOTAL $	

NOTES

AMOUNT TO SPEND
$
SPENT
$
SAVINGS
$
LEFT OVER AMOUNT
$

WEEKLY BUDGET TRACKER

WEEK OF:

MONDAY

DESCRIPTION	AMOUNT
TOTAL $	

TUESDAY

DESCRIPTION	AMOUNT
TOTAL $	

WEDNESDAY

DESCRIPTION	AMOUNT
TOTAL $	

THURSDAY

DESCRIPTION	AMOUNT
TOTAL $	

FRIDAY	
DESCRIPTION	AMOUNT
TOTAL $	

SATURDAY	
DESCRIPTION	AMOUNT
TOTAL $	

SUNDAY	
DESCRIPTION	AMOUNT
TOTAL $	

NOTES

AMOUNT TO SPEND
$
SPENT
$
SAVINGS
$
LEFT OVER AMOUNT
$

WEEKLY BUDGET TRACKER

WEEK OF:

MONDAY	
DESCRIPTION	AMOUNT
TOTAL $	

TUESDAY	
DESCRIPTION	AMOUNT
TOTAL $	

WEDNESDAY	
DESCRIPTION	AMOUNT
TOTAL $	

THURSDAY	
DESCRIPTION	AMOUNT
TOTAL $	

FRIDAY

DESCRIPTION	AMOUNT
TOTAL $	

SATURDAY

DESCRIPTION	AMOUNT
TOTAL $	

SUNDAY

DESCRIPTION	AMOUNT
TOTAL $	

NOTES

AMOUNT TO SPEND
$
SPENT
$
SAVINGS
$
LEFT OVER AMOUNT
$

WEEKLY BUDGET TRACKER

WEEK OF:

MONDAY	
DESCRIPTION	AMOUNT
TOTAL $	

TUESDAY	
DESCRIPTION	AMOUNT
TOTAL $	

WEDNESDAY	
DESCRIPTION	AMOUNT
TOTAL $	

THURSDAY	
DESCRIPTION	AMOUNT
TOTAL $	

FRIDAY

DESCRIPTION	AMOUNT
TOTAL $	

SATURDAY

DESCRIPTION	AMOUNT
TOTAL $	

SUNDAY

DESCRIPTION	AMOUNT
TOTAL $	

NOTES

AMOUNT TO SPEND
$
SPENT
$
SAVINGS
$
LEFT OVER AMOUNT
$

WEEKLY BUDGET TRACKER

WEEK OF:

MONDAY	
DESCRIPTION	AMOUNT
TOTAL $	

TUESDAY	
DESCRIPTION	AMOUNT
TOTAL $	

WEDNESDAY	
DESCRIPTION	AMOUNT
TOTAL $	

THURSDAY	
DESCRIPTION	AMOUNT
TOTAL $	

FRIDAY	
DESCRIPTION	AMOUNT
TOTAL $	

SATURDAY	
DESCRIPTION	AMOUNT
TOTAL $	

SUNDAY	
DESCRIPTION	AMOUNT
TOTAL $	

NOTES

AMOUNT TO SPEND
$
SPENT
$
SAVINGS
$
LEFT OVER AMOUNT
$

WEEKLY BUDGET TRACKER

WEEK OF:

MONDAY	
DESCRIPTION	AMOUNT
TOTAL $	

TUESDAY	
DESCRIPTION	AMOUNT
TOTAL $	

WEDNESDAY	
DESCRIPTION	AMOUNT
TOTAL $	

THURSDAY	
DESCRIPTION	AMOUNT
TOTAL $	

FRIDAY	
DESCRIPTION	AMOUNT
TOTAL $	

SATURDAY	
DESCRIPTION	AMOUNT
TOTAL $	

SUNDAY	
DESCRIPTION	AMOUNT
TOTAL $	

NOTES

AMOUNT TO SPEND
$
SPENT
$
SAVINGS
$
LEFT OVER AMOUNT
$

WEEKLY BUDGET TRACKER

WEEK OF:

MONDAY	
DESCRIPTION	AMOUNT
TOTAL $	

TUESDAY	
DESCRIPTION	AMOUNT
TOTAL $	

WEDNESDAY	
DESCRIPTION	AMOUNT
TOTAL $	

THURSDAY	
DESCRIPTION	AMOUNT
TOTAL $	

FRIDAY	
DESCRIPTION	AMOUNT
TOTAL $	

SATURDAY	
DESCRIPTION	AMOUNT
TOTAL $	

SUNDAY	
DESCRIPTION	AMOUNT
TOTAL $	

NOTES

AMOUNT TO SPEND
$
SPENT
$
SAVINGS
$
LEFT OVER AMOUNT
$

WEEKLY BUDGET TRACKER

WEEK OF:

MONDAY	
DESCRIPTION	AMOUNT
TOTAL $	

TUESDAY	
DESCRIPTION	AMOUNT
TOTAL $	

WEDNESDAY	
DESCRIPTION	AMOUNT
TOTAL $	

THURSDAY	
DESCRIPTION	AMOUNT
TOTAL $	

FRIDAY

DESCRIPTION	AMOUNT
TOTAL $	

SATURDAY

DESCRIPTION	AMOUNT
TOTAL $	

SUNDAY

DESCRIPTION	AMOUNT
TOTAL $	

NOTES

AMOUNT TO SPEND
$
SPENT
$
SAVINGS
$
LEFT OVER AMOUNT
$

WEEKLY BUDGET TRACKER

WEEK OF:

MONDAY	
DESCRIPTION	AMOUNT
TOTAL $	

TUESDAY	
DESCRIPTION	AMOUNT
TOTAL $	

WEDNESDAY	
DESCRIPTION	AMOUNT
TOTAL $	

THURSDAY	
DESCRIPTION	AMOUNT
TOTAL $	

FRIDAY	
DESCRIPTION	AMOUNT
TOTAL $	

SATURDAY	
DESCRIPTION	AMOUNT
TOTAL $	

SUNDAY	
DESCRIPTION	AMOUNT
TOTAL $	

NOTES

AMOUNT TO SPEND
$
SPENT
$
SAVINGS
$
LEFT OVER AMOUNT
$

WEEKLY BUDGET TRACKER

WEEK OF:

MONDAY

DESCRIPTION	AMOUNT
TOTAL $	

TUESDAY

DESCRIPTION	AMOUNT
TOTAL $	

WEDNESDAY

DESCRIPTION	AMOUNT
TOTAL $	

THURSDAY

DESCRIPTION	AMOUNT
TOTAL $	

FRIDAY	
DESCRIPTION	AMOUNT
TOTAL $	

SATURDAY	
DESCRIPTION	AMOUNT
TOTAL $	

SUNDAY	
DESCRIPTION	AMOUNT
TOTAL $	

NOTES

AMOUNT TO SPEND
$
SPENT
$
SAVINGS
$
LEFT OVER AMOUNT
$

WEEKLY BUDGET TRACKER

WEEK OF:

MONDAY	
DESCRIPTION	AMOUNT
TOTAL $	

TUESDAY	
DESCRIPTION	AMOUNT
TOTAL $	

WEDNESDAY	
DESCRIPTION	AMOUNT
TOTAL $	

THURSDAY	
DESCRIPTION	AMOUNT
TOTAL $	

FRIDAY	
DESCRIPTION	AMOUNT
TOTAL $	

SATURDAY	
DESCRIPTION	AMOUNT
TOTAL $	

SUNDAY	
DESCRIPTION	AMOUNT
TOTAL $	

NOTES

AMOUNT TO SPEND
$
SPENT
$
SAVINGS
$
LEFT OVER AMOUNT
$

WEEKLY BUDGET TRACKER

WEEK OF:

MONDAY	
DESCRIPTION	AMOUNT
TOTAL $	

TUESDAY	
DESCRIPTION	AMOUNT
TOTAL $	

WEDNESDAY	
DESCRIPTION	AMOUNT
TOTAL $	

THURSDAY	
DESCRIPTION	AMOUNT
TOTAL $	

FRIDAY	
DESCRIPTION	AMOUNT
TOTAL $	

SATURDAY	
DESCRIPTION	AMOUNT
TOTAL $	

SUNDAY	
DESCRIPTION	AMOUNT
TOTAL $	

NOTES

AMOUNT TO SPEND
$
SPENT
$
SAVINGS
$
LEFT OVER AMOUNT
$

WEEKLY BUDGET TRACKER

WEEK OF:

MONDAY	
DESCRIPTION	AMOUNT
TOTAL $	

TUESDAY	
DESCRIPTION	AMOUNT
TOTAL $	

WEDNESDAY	
DESCRIPTION	AMOUNT
TOTAL $	

THURSDAY	
DESCRIPTION	AMOUNT
TOTAL $	

FRIDAY	
DESCRIPTION	AMOUNT
TOTAL $	

SATURDAY	
DESCRIPTION	AMOUNT
TOTAL $	

SUNDAY	
DESCRIPTION	AMOUNT
TOTAL $	

NOTES

AMOUNT TO SPEND

$

SPENT

$

SAVINGS

$

LEFT OVER AMOUNT

$

WEEKLY BUDGET TRACKER

WEEK OF:

MONDAY	
DESCRIPTION	AMOUNT
TOTAL $	

TUESDAY	
DESCRIPTION	AMOUNT
TOTAL $	

WEDNESDAY	
DESCRIPTION	AMOUNT
TOTAL $	

THURSDAY	
DESCRIPTION	AMOUNT
TOTAL $	

FRIDAY	
DESCRIPTION	AMOUNT
TOTAL $	

SATURDAY	
DESCRIPTION	AMOUNT
TOTAL $	

SUNDAY	
DESCRIPTION	AMOUNT
TOTAL $	

NOTES

AMOUNT TO SPEND
$
SPENT
$
SAVINGS
$
LEFT OVER AMOUNT
$

WEEKLY BUDGET TRACKER

WEEK OF:

MONDAY

DESCRIPTION	AMOUNT
TOTAL $	

TUESDAY

DESCRIPTION	AMOUNT
TOTAL $	

WEDNESDAY

DESCRIPTION	AMOUNT
TOTAL $	

THURSDAY

DESCRIPTION	AMOUNT
TOTAL $	

FRIDAY	
DESCRIPTION	AMOUNT
TOTAL $	

SATURDAY	
DESCRIPTION	AMOUNT
TOTAL $	

SUNDAY	
DESCRIPTION	AMOUNT
TOTAL $	

NOTES

AMOUNT TO SPEND
$
SPENT
$
SAVINGS
$
LEFT OVER AMOUNT
$

WEEKLY BUDGET TRACKER

WEEK OF:

MONDAY	
DESCRIPTION	AMOUNT
TOTAL $	

TUESDAY	
DESCRIPTION	AMOUNT
TOTAL $	

WEDNESDAY	
DESCRIPTION	AMOUNT
TOTAL $	

THURSDAY	
DESCRIPTION	AMOUNT
TOTAL $	

FRIDAY	
DESCRIPTION	AMOUNT
TOTAL $	

SATURDAY	
DESCRIPTION	AMOUNT
TOTAL $	

SUNDAY	
DESCRIPTION	AMOUNT
TOTAL $	

NOTES

AMOUNT TO SPEND
$
SPENT
$
SAVINGS
$
LEFT OVER AMOUNT
$

WEEKLY BUDGET TRACKER

WEEK OF:

MONDAY	
DESCRIPTION	AMOUNT
TOTAL $	

TUESDAY	
DESCRIPTION	AMOUNT
TOTAL $	

WEDNESDAY	
DESCRIPTION	AMOUNT
TOTAL $	

THURSDAY	
DESCRIPTION	AMOUNT
TOTAL $	

FRIDAY

DESCRIPTION	AMOUNT
TOTAL $	

SATURDAY

DESCRIPTION	AMOUNT
TOTAL $	

SUNDAY

DESCRIPTION	AMOUNT
TOTAL $	

NOTES

AMOUNT TO SPEND
$
SPENT
$
SAVINGS
$
LEFT OVER AMOUNT
$

WEEKLY BUDGET TRACKER

WEEK OF:

MONDAY	
DESCRIPTION	AMOUNT
TOTAL $	

TUESDAY	
DESCRIPTION	AMOUNT
TOTAL $	

WEDNESDAY	
DESCRIPTION	AMOUNT
TOTAL $	

THURSDAY	
DESCRIPTION	AMOUNT
TOTAL $	

FRIDAY

DESCRIPTION	AMOUNT
TOTAL $	

SATURDAY

DESCRIPTION	AMOUNT
TOTAL $	

SUNDAY

DESCRIPTION	AMOUNT
TOTAL $	

NOTES

AMOUNT TO SPEND
$
SPENT
$
SAVINGS
$
LEFT OVER AMOUNT
$

WEEKLY BUDGET TRACKER

WEEK OF:

MONDAY

DESCRIPTION	AMOUNT
TOTAL $	

TUESDAY

DESCRIPTION	AMOUNT
TOTAL $	

WEDNESDAY

DESCRIPTION	AMOUNT
TOTAL $	

THURSDAY

DESCRIPTION	AMOUNT
TOTAL $	

FRIDAY

DESCRIPTION	AMOUNT
TOTAL $	

SATURDAY

DESCRIPTION	AMOUNT
TOTAL $	

SUNDAY

DESCRIPTION	AMOUNT
TOTAL $	

NOTES

AMOUNT TO SPEND
$
SPENT
$
SAVINGS
$
LEFT OVER AMOUNT
$

WEEKLY BUDGET TRACKER

WEEK OF:

MONDAY	
DESCRIPTION	AMOUNT
TOTAL $	

TUESDAY	
DESCRIPTION	AMOUNT
TOTAL $	

WEDNESDAY	
DESCRIPTION	AMOUNT
TOTAL $	

THURSDAY	
DESCRIPTION	AMOUNT
TOTAL $	

FRIDAY

DESCRIPTION	AMOUNT
TOTAL $	

SATURDAY

DESCRIPTION	AMOUNT
TOTAL $	

SUNDAY

DESCRIPTION	AMOUNT
TOTAL $	

NOTES

AMOUNT TO SPEND
$
SPENT
$
SAVINGS
$
LEFT OVER AMOUNT
$

WEEKLY BUDGET TRACKER

WEEK OF:

MONDAY	
DESCRIPTION	AMOUNT
TOTAL $	

TUESDAY	
DESCRIPTION	AMOUNT
TOTAL $	

WEDNESDAY	
DESCRIPTION	AMOUNT
TOTAL $	

THURSDAY	
DESCRIPTION	AMOUNT
TOTAL $	

FRIDAY	
DESCRIPTION	AMOUNT
TOTAL $	

SATURDAY	
DESCRIPTION	AMOUNT
TOTAL $	

SUNDAY	
DESCRIPTION	AMOUNT
TOTAL $	

NOTES

AMOUNT TO SPEND
$
SPENT
$
SAVINGS
$
LEFT OVER AMOUNT
$

WEEKLY BUDGET TRACKER

WEEK OF:

MONDAY	
DESCRIPTION	AMOUNT
TOTAL $	

TUESDAY	
DESCRIPTION	AMOUNT
TOTAL $	

WEDNESDAY	
DESCRIPTION	AMOUNT
TOTAL $	

THURSDAY	
DESCRIPTION	AMOUNT
TOTAL $	

FRIDAY	
DESCRIPTION	AMOUNT
TOTAL $	

SATURDAY	
DESCRIPTION	AMOUNT
TOTAL $	

SUNDAY	
DESCRIPTION	AMOUNT
TOTAL $	

NOTES

AMOUNT TO SPEND
$
SPENT
$
SAVINGS
$
LEFT OVER AMOUNT
$

WEEKLY BUDGET TRACKER

WEEK OF:

MONDAY	
DESCRIPTION	AMOUNT
TOTAL $	

TUESDAY	
DESCRIPTION	AMOUNT
TOTAL $	

WEDNESDAY	
DESCRIPTION	AMOUNT
TOTAL $	

THURSDAY	
DESCRIPTION	AMOUNT
TOTAL $	

FRIDAY	
DESCRIPTION	AMOUNT
TOTAL $	

SATURDAY	
DESCRIPTION	AMOUNT
TOTAL $	

SUNDAY	
DESCRIPTION	AMOUNT
TOTAL $	

NOTES

AMOUNT TO SPEND
$
SPENT
$
SAVINGS
$
LEFT OVER AMOUNT
$

WEEKLY BUDGET TRACKER

WEEK OF:

MONDAY

DESCRIPTION	AMOUNT
TOTAL $	

TUESDAY

DESCRIPTION	AMOUNT
TOTAL $	

WEDNESDAY

DESCRIPTION	AMOUNT
TOTAL $	

THURSDAY

DESCRIPTION	AMOUNT
TOTAL $	

FRIDAY	
DESCRIPTION	AMOUNT
TOTAL $	

SATURDAY	
DESCRIPTION	AMOUNT
TOTAL $	

SUNDAY	
DESCRIPTION	AMOUNT
TOTAL $	

NOTES

AMOUNT TO SPEND
$
SPENT
$
SAVINGS
$
LEFT OVER AMOUNT
$

WEEKLY BUDGET TRACKER

WEEK OF:

MONDAY	
DESCRIPTION	AMOUNT
TOTAL $	

TUESDAY	
DESCRIPTION	AMOUNT
TOTAL $	

WEDNESDAY	
DESCRIPTION	AMOUNT
TOTAL $	

THURSDAY	
DESCRIPTION	AMOUNT
TOTAL $	

FRIDAY

DESCRIPTION	AMOUNT
TOTAL $	

SATURDAY

DESCRIPTION	AMOUNT
TOTAL $	

SUNDAY

DESCRIPTION	AMOUNT
TOTAL $	

NOTES

AMOUNT TO SPEND
$
SPENT
$
SAVINGS
$
LEFT OVER AMOUNT
$

WEEKLY BUDGET TRACKER

WEEK OF:

MONDAY	
DESCRIPTION	AMOUNT
TOTAL $	

TUESDAY	
DESCRIPTION	AMOUNT
TOTAL $	

WEDNESDAY	
DESCRIPTION	AMOUNT
TOTAL $	

THURSDAY	
DESCRIPTION	AMOUNT
TOTAL $	

FRIDAY

DESCRIPTION	AMOUNT
TOTAL $	

SATURDAY

DESCRIPTION	AMOUNT
TOTAL $	

SUNDAY

DESCRIPTION	AMOUNT
TOTAL $	

NOTES

AMOUNT TO SPEND
$
SPENT
$
SAVINGS
$
LEFT OVER AMOUNT
$

WEEKLY BUDGET TRACKER

WEEK OF:

MONDAY

DESCRIPTION	AMOUNT
TOTAL $	

TUESDAY

DESCRIPTION	AMOUNT
TOTAL $	

WEDNESDAY

DESCRIPTION	AMOUNT
TOTAL $	

THURSDAY

DESCRIPTION	AMOUNT
TOTAL $	

FRIDAY	
DESCRIPTION	AMOUNT
TOTAL $	

SATURDAY	
DESCRIPTION	AMOUNT
TOTAL $	

SUNDAY	
DESCRIPTION	AMOUNT
TOTAL $	

NOTES

AMOUNT TO SPEND
$
SPENT
$
SAVINGS
$
LEFT OVER AMOUNT
$

WEEKLY BUDGET TRACKER

WEEK OF:

MONDAY

DESCRIPTION	AMOUNT
TOTAL $	

TUESDAY

DESCRIPTION	AMOUNT
TOTAL $	

WEDNESDAY

DESCRIPTION	AMOUNT
TOTAL $	

THURSDAY

DESCRIPTION	AMOUNT
TOTAL $	

FRIDAY	
DESCRIPTION	AMOUNT
TOTAL $	

SATURDAY	
DESCRIPTION	AMOUNT
TOTAL $	

SUNDAY	
DESCRIPTION	AMOUNT
TOTAL $	

NOTES

AMOUNT TO SPEND
$
SPENT
$
SAVINGS
$
LEFT OVER AMOUNT
$

WEEKLY BUDGET TRACKER

WEEK OF:

MONDAY	
DESCRIPTION	AMOUNT
TOTAL $	

TUESDAY	
DESCRIPTION	AMOUNT
TOTAL $	

WEDNESDAY	
DESCRIPTION	AMOUNT
TOTAL $	

THURSDAY	
DESCRIPTION	AMOUNT
TOTAL $	

FRIDAY

DESCRIPTION	AMOUNT
TOTAL $	

SATURDAY

DESCRIPTION	AMOUNT
TOTAL $	

SUNDAY

DESCRIPTION	AMOUNT
TOTAL $	

NOTES

AMOUNT TO SPEND
$
SPENT
$
SAVINGS
$
LEFT OVER AMOUNT
$

WEEKLY BUDGET TRACKER

WEEK OF:

MONDAY	
DESCRIPTION	AMOUNT
TOTAL $	

TUESDAY	
DESCRIPTION	AMOUNT
TOTAL $	

WEDNESDAY	
DESCRIPTION	AMOUNT
TOTAL $	

THURSDAY	
DESCRIPTION	AMOUNT
TOTAL $	

FRIDAY

DESCRIPTION	AMOUNT
TOTAL $	

SATURDAY

DESCRIPTION	AMOUNT
TOTAL $	

SUNDAY

DESCRIPTION	AMOUNT
TOTAL $	

NOTES

AMOUNT TO SPEND
$
SPENT
$
SAVINGS
$
LEFT OVER AMOUNT
$

WEEKLY BUDGET TRACKER

WEEK OF:

MONDAY	
DESCRIPTION	AMOUNT
TOTAL $	

TUESDAY	
DESCRIPTION	AMOUNT
TOTAL $	

WEDNESDAY	
DESCRIPTION	AMOUNT
TOTAL $	

THURSDAY	
DESCRIPTION	AMOUNT
TOTAL $	

FRIDAY	
DESCRIPTION	AMOUNT
TOTAL $	

SATURDAY	
DESCRIPTION	AMOUNT
TOTAL $	

SUNDAY	
DESCRIPTION	AMOUNT
TOTAL $	

NOTES

AMOUNT TO SPEND
$
SPENT
$
SAVINGS
$
LEFT OVER AMOUNT
$

WEEKLY BUDGET TRACKER

WEEK OF:

MONDAY	
DESCRIPTION	AMOUNT
TOTAL $	

TUESDAY	
DESCRIPTION	AMOUNT
TOTAL $	

WEDNESDAY	
DESCRIPTION	AMOUNT
TOTAL $	

THURSDAY	
DESCRIPTION	AMOUNT
TOTAL $	

FRIDAY	
DESCRIPTION	AMOUNT
TOTAL $	

SATURDAY	
DESCRIPTION	AMOUNT
TOTAL $	

SUNDAY	
DESCRIPTION	AMOUNT
TOTAL $	

NOTES

AMOUNT TO SPEND
$
SPENT
$
SAVINGS
$
LEFT OVER AMOUNT
$

WEEKLY BUDGET TRACKER

WEEK OF:

MONDAY

DESCRIPTION	AMOUNT
TOTAL $	

TUESDAY

DESCRIPTION	AMOUNT
TOTAL $	

WEDNESDAY

DESCRIPTION	AMOUNT
TOTAL $	

THURSDAY

DESCRIPTION	AMOUNT
TOTAL $	

FRIDAY	
DESCRIPTION	AMOUNT
TOTAL $	

SATURDAY	
DESCRIPTION	AMOUNT
TOTAL $	

SUNDAY	
DESCRIPTION	AMOUNT
TOTAL $	

NOTES

AMOUNT TO SPEND
$
SPENT
$
SAVINGS
$
LEFT OVER AMOUNT
$

WEEKLY BUDGET TRACKER

WEEK OF:

MONDAY	
DESCRIPTION	AMOUNT
TOTAL $	

TUESDAY	
DESCRIPTION	AMOUNT
TOTAL $	

WEDNESDAY	
DESCRIPTION	AMOUNT
TOTAL $	

THURSDAY	
DESCRIPTION	AMOUNT
TOTAL $	

FRIDAY

DESCRIPTION	AMOUNT
TOTAL $	

SATURDAY

DESCRIPTION	AMOUNT
TOTAL $	

SUNDAY

DESCRIPTION	AMOUNT
TOTAL $	

NOTES

AMOUNT TO SPEND
$
SPENT
$
SAVINGS
$
LEFT OVER AMOUNT
$

WEEKLY BUDGET TRACKER

WEEK OF:

MONDAY	
DESCRIPTION	AMOUNT
TOTAL $	

TUESDAY	
DESCRIPTION	AMOUNT
TOTAL $	

WEDNESDAY	
DESCRIPTION	AMOUNT
TOTAL $	

THURSDAY	
DESCRIPTION	AMOUNT
TOTAL $	

FRIDAY	
DESCRIPTION	AMOUNT
TOTAL $	

SATURDAY	
DESCRIPTION	AMOUNT
TOTAL $	

SUNDAY	
DESCRIPTION	AMOUNT
TOTAL $	

NOTES

AMOUNT TO SPEND
$
SPENT
$
SAVINGS
$
LEFT OVER AMOUNT
$

WEEKLY BUDGET TRACKER

WEEK OF:

MONDAY	
DESCRIPTION	AMOUNT
TOTAL $	

TUESDAY	
DESCRIPTION	AMOUNT
TOTAL $	

WEDNESDAY	
DESCRIPTION	AMOUNT
TOTAL $	

THURSDAY	
DESCRIPTION	AMOUNT
TOTAL $	

FRIDAY	
DESCRIPTION	AMOUNT
TOTAL $	

SATURDAY	
DESCRIPTION	AMOUNT
TOTAL $	

SUNDAY	
DESCRIPTION	AMOUNT
TOTAL $	

NOTES

AMOUNT TO SPEND
$
SPENT
$
SAVINGS
$
LEFT OVER AMOUNT
$

WEEKLY BUDGET TRACKER

WEEK OF:

MONDAY	
DESCRIPTION	AMOUNT
TOTAL $	

TUESDAY	
DESCRIPTION	AMOUNT
TOTAL $	

WEDNESDAY	
DESCRIPTION	AMOUNT
TOTAL $	

THURSDAY	
DESCRIPTION	AMOUNT
TOTAL $	

FRIDAY	
DESCRIPTION	AMOUNT
TOTAL $	

SATURDAY	
DESCRIPTION	AMOUNT
TOTAL $	

SUNDAY	
DESCRIPTION	AMOUNT
TOTAL $	

NOTES

AMOUNT TO SPEND
$
SPENT
$
SAVINGS
$
LEFT OVER AMOUNT
$

WEEKLY BUDGET TRACKER

WEEK OF:

MONDAY	
DESCRIPTION	AMOUNT
TOTAL $	

TUESDAY	
DESCRIPTION	AMOUNT
TOTAL $	

WEDNESDAY	
DESCRIPTION	AMOUNT
TOTAL $	

THURSDAY	
DESCRIPTION	AMOUNT
TOTAL $	

FRIDAY	
DESCRIPTION	AMOUNT
TOTAL $	

SATURDAY	
DESCRIPTION	AMOUNT
TOTAL $	

SUNDAY	
DESCRIPTION	AMOUNT
TOTAL $	

NOTES

AMOUNT TO SPEND
$
SPENT
$
SAVINGS
$
LEFT OVER AMOUNT
$

WEEKLY BUDGET TRACKER

WEEK OF:

MONDAY	
DESCRIPTION	AMOUNT
TOTAL $	

TUESDAY	
DESCRIPTION	AMOUNT
TOTAL $	

WEDNESDAY	
DESCRIPTION	AMOUNT
TOTAL $	

THURSDAY	
DESCRIPTION	AMOUNT
TOTAL $	

FRIDAY	
DESCRIPTION	AMOUNT
TOTAL $	

SATURDAY	
DESCRIPTION	AMOUNT
TOTAL $	

SUNDAY	
DESCRIPTION	AMOUNT
TOTAL $	

NOTES

AMOUNT TO SPEND
$
SPENT
$
SAVINGS
$
LEFT OVER AMOUNT
$

WEEKLY BUDGET TRACKER

WEEK OF:

MONDAY	
DESCRIPTION	AMOUNT
TOTAL $	

TUESDAY	
DESCRIPTION	AMOUNT
TOTAL $	

WEDNESDAY	
DESCRIPTION	AMOUNT
TOTAL $	

THURSDAY	
DESCRIPTION	AMOUNT
TOTAL $	

FRIDAY

DESCRIPTION	AMOUNT
TOTAL $	

SATURDAY

DESCRIPTION	AMOUNT
TOTAL $	

SUNDAY

DESCRIPTION	AMOUNT
TOTAL $	

NOTES

AMOUNT TO SPEND
$
SPENT
$
SAVINGS
$
LEFT OVER AMOUNT
$

WEEKLY BUDGET TRACKER

WEEK OF:

MONDAY	
DESCRIPTION	AMOUNT
TOTAL $	

TUESDAY	
DESCRIPTION	AMOUNT
TOTAL $	

WEDNESDAY	
DESCRIPTION	AMOUNT
TOTAL $	

THURSDAY	
DESCRIPTION	AMOUNT
TOTAL $	

FRIDAY	
DESCRIPTION	AMOUNT
TOTAL $	

SATURDAY	
DESCRIPTION	AMOUNT
TOTAL $	

SUNDAY	
DESCRIPTION	AMOUNT
TOTAL $	

NOTES

AMOUNT TO SPEND
$
SPENT
$
SAVINGS
$
LEFT OVER AMOUNT
$

WEEKLY BUDGET TRACKER

WEEK OF:

MONDAY	
DESCRIPTION	AMOUNT
TOTAL $	

TUESDAY	
DESCRIPTION	AMOUNT
TOTAL $	

WEDNESDAY	
DESCRIPTION	AMOUNT
TOTAL $	

THURSDAY	
DESCRIPTION	AMOUNT
TOTAL $	

FRIDAY	
DESCRIPTION	AMOUNT
TOTAL $	

SATURDAY	
DESCRIPTION	AMOUNT
TOTAL $	

SUNDAY	
DESCRIPTION	AMOUNT
TOTAL $	

NOTES

AMOUNT TO SPEND
$
SPENT
$
SAVINGS
$
LEFT OVER AMOUNT
$

WEEKLY BUDGET TRACKER

WEEK OF:

MONDAY	
DESCRIPTION	AMOUNT
TOTAL $	

TUESDAY	
DESCRIPTION	AMOUNT
TOTAL $	

WEDNESDAY	
DESCRIPTION	AMOUNT
TOTAL $	

THURSDAY	
DESCRIPTION	AMOUNT
TOTAL $	

FRIDAY	
DESCRIPTION	AMOUNT
TOTAL $	

SATURDAY	
DESCRIPTION	AMOUNT
TOTAL $	

SUNDAY	
DESCRIPTION	AMOUNT
TOTAL $	

NOTES

AMOUNT TO SPEND
$
SPENT
$
SAVINGS
$
LEFT OVER AMOUNT
$

WEEKLY BUDGET TRACKER

WEEK OF:

MONDAY

DESCRIPTION	AMOUNT
TOTAL $	

TUESDAY

DESCRIPTION	AMOUNT
TOTAL $	

WEDNESDAY

DESCRIPTION	AMOUNT
TOTAL $	

THURSDAY

DESCRIPTION	AMOUNT
TOTAL $	

FRIDAY	
DESCRIPTION	AMOUNT
TOTAL $	

SATURDAY	
DESCRIPTION	AMOUNT
TOTAL $	

SUNDAY	
DESCRIPTION	AMOUNT
TOTAL $	

NOTES

AMOUNT TO SPEND
$
SPENT
$
SAVINGS
$
LEFT OVER AMOUNT
$

WEEKLY BUDGET TRACKER

WEEK OF:

MONDAY	
DESCRIPTION	AMOUNT
TOTAL $	

TUESDAY	
DESCRIPTION	AMOUNT
TOTAL $	

WEDNESDAY	
DESCRIPTION	AMOUNT
TOTAL $	

THURSDAY	
DESCRIPTION	AMOUNT
TOTAL $	

FRIDAY	
DESCRIPTION	AMOUNT
TOTAL $	

SATURDAY	
DESCRIPTION	AMOUNT
TOTAL $	

SUNDAY	
DESCRIPTION	AMOUNT
TOTAL $	

NOTES

AMOUNT TO SPEND
$
SPENT
$
SAVINGS
$
LEFT OVER AMOUNT
$

WEEKLY BUDGET TRACKER

WEEK OF:

MONDAY

DESCRIPTION	AMOUNT
TOTAL $	

TUESDAY

DESCRIPTION	AMOUNT
TOTAL $	

WEDNESDAY

DESCRIPTION	AMOUNT
TOTAL $	

THURSDAY

DESCRIPTION	AMOUNT
TOTAL $	

FRIDAY	
DESCRIPTION	AMOUNT
TOTAL $	

SATURDAY	
DESCRIPTION	AMOUNT
TOTAL $	

SUNDAY	
DESCRIPTION	AMOUNT
TOTAL $	

NOTES

AMOUNT TO SPEND
$
SPENT
$
SAVINGS
$
LEFT OVER AMOUNT
$

WEEKLY BUDGET TRACKER

WEEK OF:

MONDAY

DESCRIPTION	AMOUNT
TOTAL $	

TUESDAY

DESCRIPTION	AMOUNT
TOTAL $	

WEDNESDAY

DESCRIPTION	AMOUNT
TOTAL $	

THURSDAY

DESCRIPTION	AMOUNT
TOTAL $	

FRIDAY	
DESCRIPTION	AMOUNT
TOTAL $	

SATURDAY	
DESCRIPTION	AMOUNT
TOTAL $	

SUNDAY	
DESCRIPTION	AMOUNT
TOTAL $	

NOTES

AMOUNT TO SPEND
$
SPENT
$
SAVINGS
$
LEFT OVER AMOUNT
$

WEEKLY BUDGET TRACKER

WEEK OF:

MONDAY	
DESCRIPTION	AMOUNT
TOTAL $	

TUESDAY	
DESCRIPTION	AMOUNT
TOTAL $	

WEDNESDAY	
DESCRIPTION	AMOUNT
TOTAL $	

THURSDAY	
DESCRIPTION	AMOUNT
TOTAL $	

FRIDAY	
DESCRIPTION	AMOUNT
TOTAL $	

SATURDAY	
DESCRIPTION	AMOUNT
TOTAL $	

SUNDAY	
DESCRIPTION	AMOUNT
TOTAL $	

NOTES

AMOUNT TO SPEND
$
SPENT
$
SAVINGS
$
LEFT OVER AMOUNT
$

WEEKLY BUDGET TRACKER

WEEK OF:

MONDAY

DESCRIPTION	AMOUNT
TOTAL $	

TUESDAY

DESCRIPTION	AMOUNT
TOTAL $	

WEDNESDAY

DESCRIPTION	AMOUNT
TOTAL $	

THURSDAY

DESCRIPTION	AMOUNT
TOTAL $	

FRIDAY	
DESCRIPTION	AMOUNT
TOTAL $	

SATURDAY	
DESCRIPTION	AMOUNT
TOTAL $	

SUNDAY	
DESCRIPTION	AMOUNT
TOTAL $	

NOTES

AMOUNT TO SPEND
$
SPENT
$
SAVINGS
$
LEFT OVER AMOUNT
$

WEEKLY BUDGET TRACKER

WEEK OF:

MONDAY	
DESCRIPTION	AMOUNT
TOTAL $	

TUESDAY	
DESCRIPTION	AMOUNT
TOTAL $	

WEDNESDAY	
DESCRIPTION	AMOUNT
TOTAL $	

THURSDAY	
DESCRIPTION	AMOUNT
TOTAL $	

FRIDAY	
DESCRIPTION	AMOUNT
TOTAL $	

SATURDAY	
DESCRIPTION	AMOUNT
TOTAL $	

SUNDAY	
DESCRIPTION	AMOUNT
TOTAL $	

NOTES

AMOUNT TO SPEND
$
SPENT
$
SAVINGS
$
LEFT OVER AMOUNT
$

Made in the USA
Monee, IL
08 November 2026

67967208R00111